Purpose of Primer

This primer illustrates some of the connections and workflows that can exist in North Carolina's elder protection system. This is not a comprehensive review of every possible action, option, or remedy available to help older adults who are victims of abuse, neglect, or exploitation. Rather, this primer is a summary-level snapshot that should be used in conjunction with the *Legal Framework for North Carolina's Elder Protection System (Legal Framework)* and the companion website protectadults.sog.unc.edu, which are more comprehensive resources.

In the center of this primer is a color-coded flowchart illustrating the potential connectivity among several key actors in the elder protection system:

- **Red: Adult Protective Services**
- **Green: Clerks of Superior Court**
- **Blue: Law Enforcement**
- **Grey: Financial Institutions**

Please note that this flowchart is an overly simplified representation of a complex and multi-faceted system. Elder protection involves many more actors, such as private attorneys, nonprofit organizations, health care providers, state and federal agencies, and others. In the *Legal Framework*, an entire chapter focuses on powers of attorney (Chapter 5). Another chapter discusses the role of private civil remedies, such as civil actions for monetary relief or rescission of documents, protective orders, and housing-related actions (Chapter 6). Chapter 7 briefly summarizes the various roles that health care providers, state agencies, federal agencies, and others play in the elder protection system.

A more detailed, interactive version of the flowchart is included on the project website.

Key Terms

Several key terms are used frequently throughout this primer and more generally in the elder protection community. A few of these terms are highlighted and defined below to help guide readers as they navigate both the roadmap and the accompanying text.

ADULT PROTECTIVE SERVICES (APS)

In North Carolina, the term "protective services" is defined broadly to encompass the process of evaluating a disabled adult's needs and mobilizing those services necessary to protect the adult from abuse, neglect, or exploitation. (G.S. 108A-101(n).) This definition is intentionally vague because the circumstances in each APS case are unique, and the needs will vary tremendously from person to person.

DISABLED ADULT

Under state APS laws, a "disabled adult" is a person who is

- 18 years of age or older or a lawfully emancipated minor,
- present in the state of North Carolina, and
- physically or mentally incapacitated.

A person may be physically or mentally incapacitated as a result of "an intellectual disability, cerebral palsy, epilepsy or autism; organic brain damage caused by advanced age or other physical degeneration in connection therewith; or due to conditions incurred at any age which are the result of accident, organic brain damage, mental or physical illness, or continued consumption or absorption of substances." (G.S. 108A-101(d).)

ELDER ABUSE

The term "elder abuse" is not defined in North Carolina law. This primer and the related resources rely primarily on the definition published by the U.S. Centers for Disease Control and Prevention. That definition generally encompasses an intentional act, or a failure to act, by a caregiver or another person in a relationship involving an expectation of trust that causes or creates a risk of harm to an older adult.

GUARDIANSHIP

Guardianship is the legal relationship created by a state court that gives a person or entity (the guardian) the authority to make decisions for an individual who lacks capacity (the ward) with respect to the individual's personal affairs, financial affairs, or both.

INCOMPETENT ADULT

The term "incompetent adult" is defined under North Carolina law as an adult or emancipated minor who lacks sufficient capacity to either

- manage his or her own affairs or
- make or communicate important decisions concerning his or her person, family, or property

whether the lack of capacity is due to mental illness, intellectual disability, epilepsy, cerebral palsy, autism, inebriety, senility, disease, injury, or similar cause or condition. (G.S. 35A-1101(7).)

OLDER ADULT

In North Carolina, some laws recognize adults over 60 as "older," while others focus on adults over 65. Some laws, such as those covering APS and guardianship, apply more generally to all adults but are triggered only if the adult is disabled (APS) or incompetent (guardianship).

General Background

The roadmap at the center of this primer provides a high-level overview of the elder protection system. In order to help explain some of the context for the various points on the roadmap, excerpts from the Legal Framework are included below. In addition, each section below includes cross references to the relevant sections of the Legal Framework to allow for further exploration of the topic highlighted.

REPORT MADE TO DSS

There is one universal APS reporting requirement in state law: Any person who has reasonable cause to believe that a disabled adult is in need of protective services must make a report to the county department of social services (DSS). (G.S. 108A-102(a).) With one exception, this reporting requirement applies to everyone—including law enforcement officials, court officials, and health care providers. Regional staff working with the State Long-Term Care Ombudsman Program, which provides advocacy for long-term care facility residents, are excepted from the mandatory reporting requirement. They are allowed to report abuse, neglect, or exploitation to APS with the consent of the long-term care resident or the State Ombudsman.

There are also two more narrowly tailored reporting requirements that apply to the following organizations and individuals:

- Financial Institutions, including officers and employees (G.S. 108A-115.)
- Employees and volunteers at mental health, developmental disability, or substance abuse treatment facilities (MH/DD/SA) (G.S. 122C-66.)

Legal Framework, Chapter 2, Section II.C.1.

DSS SCREENS THE REPORT TO DETERMINE IF APS HAS AUTHORITY

When DSS receives a report, APS staff is required to screen the report to determine whether it falls within the scope of DSS's authority. In some circumstances, DSS may screen out a report because the agency does not have legal authority under the protective services law to take action. There are three types of situations in which DSS lacks the authority to proceed with the provision of protective services:

- The adult is not "disabled," as defined by state law;
- A responsible person is able and willing to help the adult; or
- Alleged abuse or neglect is being inflicted by someone other than a caretaker.

If DSS decides to screen out a case, the agency will not continue pursuing protective services but may connect the adult with other services and supports, make a referral to a civil attorney who could help assess whether to seek monetary damages or other relief (*Legal Framework*, Ch. 6, Section II.C), refer the case to law enforcement (Ch. 3, Section II), or refer the adult to a state or federal agency. (Ch. 7, Section II.)

Legal Framework, Chapter 2, Section II.C.2.

DSS CONDUCTS APS EVALUATION

If DSS screens in a report, the staff will conduct an evaluation to determine whether the adult is "in need of protective services." The term "protective services" means "services provided by the state or other government or private organizations or individuals which are necessary to protect the disabled adult from abuse, neglect, or exploitation. They shall consist of evaluation of the need for service and mobilization of essential services on behalf of the disabled adult." (G.S. 108A-101(n).) "Essential services" are defined as "those social, medical, psychiatric, psychological or legal services necessary to safeguard the disabled adult's rights and resources and to maintain the physical or mental well-being of the individual." (G.S. 108A-101(i).) There are some examples of essential services included in the statute, such as medical care, shelter, and protection from mistreatment. But overall, these definitions are expansive and flexible, which allows DSS to develop a protective services plan tailored to the adult's specific needs.

CONSIDER

At this point in the process, think about whether an effort should be made to protect the older adult victim's assets in a financial exploitation case.

Four options to consider:

1. *If a person has been criminally charged with financial exploitation, the prosecutor may ask the court to freeze the defendant's assets. (Legal Framework, Ch. 3, Section III.G.)*
2. *If DSS is conducting an APS evaluation, it can ask the court for an order authorizing the agency to freeze the older adult's assets and inspect financial records. (Ch. 2, Section II.C.3.e.)*
3. *If the older adult victim lacks capacity, DSS may seek guardianship, including interim guardianship. (Ch. 4, Section II.C.3.b.) An interim guardian may, for example, take action to locate and secure assets and obtain financial records to the extent authorized by the court order appointing the interim guardian.*
4. *If the older adult victim has a power of attorney and lacks capacity, DSS may file a POA proceeding to remove the agent under the POA if the agent is the source of the exploitation. (Ch. 5, Section III.A.2.f.)*

If after conducting the evaluation, DSS concludes that the adult does not require protective services, the agency will not continue down that path but may offer the adult other services and supports, make a referral to a civil attorney who can seek damages or other relief on the adult's behalf (*Legal Framework*, Ch. 6, Section II.C), refer the case to law enforcement (Ch. 3, Section II), or refer the adult to a state or federal agency. (Ch. 7, Section II.)

Legal Framework, Ch. 2, Section II.C.3.

DSS MUST DETERMINE WHETHER THE ADULT HAS CAPACITY TO CONSENT TO APS

If DSS concludes that an adult needs protectives services, the agency must then determine whether the disabled adult has capacity to consent to those services. Guidance from the state explains that the focus should be on the adult's ability to perceive and understand his or her situation, including his or her physical limitations, the resources and assistance that are available to him or her, and the consequences of not getting such assistance. (N.C. Dept of Health & Human Servs., Div. of Aging & Adult Servs., Adult Protective Services Manual III-28.) It also emphasizes a few other points.

- **Capacity is different than competency.** The former is determined by DSS for the limited purpose of assessing ability to consent to services, while the latter is determined by a judicial official in the context of a guardianship case.
- **Capacity may be intermittent.** Someone with an acute illness, such as a urinary tract infection, may temporarily lack decisional capacity. Once treated, however, the person's capacity may be restored, and DSS should recognize that change and adapt to it.
- **Professional evaluations may be helpful, but they are not determinative.** If DSS is unsure about an adult's capacity, it may consult with a medical or behavioral health professional. The decision about capacity, however, rests solely with DSS.

If DSS concludes that an older adult has capacity, it must ask the adult for his or her consent to provide protective services. (G.S. 108A-104(a).) If, on the other hand, DSS concludes that the older adult lacks capacity to consent, the agency must ask a court to order it to provide these services.

If DSS concludes that an adult needs protective services but lacks the capacity to consent, the agency may file a petition in district court requesting permission to provide those services. If the court finds by clear, cogent, and convincing evidence that the disabled adult (1) is in need of protective services and (2) lacks capacity to consent, it will issue an order authorizing DSS to provide services.

e adult
may

t

DSS conducts
APS evaluation

DSS determines that
the adult needs APS

DSS must determine
whether the adult has
capacity to consent to APS

Adult lacks capacity
to consent to APS

Adult has capacity
to consent to APS

must notify
ict attorney

DSS may file for
guardianship

DSS may ask a judge
to issue an APS order

If the adult does not
consent, DSS does not
provide APS

If the adult consents,
DSS provides APS

Any Person May File for Guardianship

After petition is filed,
clerk appoints guardian
ad litem attorney

If there is an imminent risk of
harm to the older adult or the
older adult's property, the
court may appoint an interim
guardian after notice and
hearing

rt Made to DSS

If any person involved with
the guardianship process
has reasonable cause to
suspect abuse of a disabled
adult, must report to DSS

Court holds hearing to
determine whether the
older adult is incompetent

ent

If court finds adult is incompetent,
court appoints a guardian. This may
be a guardian of the estate, a
guardian of the person, or a general
guardian

If adult is not
incompetent, court
dismisses petition

Once appointed, the guardian
has a role in protecting the
older adult against abuse

In an emergency, the court may
(1) enter ex parte orders prior to
holding a hearing on a motion
filed with the court or (2) remove
the guardian without a hearing.

t oversight of guardianship can
protect older adults from
e by the guardian or others

AFTER A PETITION IS FILED, CLERK APPOINTS GUARDIAN AD LITEM ATTORNEY

Every older adult who is a respondent in an incompetency proceeding is entitled to be represented by counsel of his or her choice or by an appointed guardian ad litem attorney (GAL). (G.S. 35A-1107.) Upon the filing of a petition, the court appoints a GAL to represent the older adult. The GAL serves a dual role. The GAL's primary role is to make every reasonable effort to determine the older adult's wishes regarding the incompetency proceeding and any proposed guardianship. The GAL must present those wishes to the court at all relevant stages of the proceedings. The GAL also makes recommendations to the clerk regarding the older adult's best interests, to the extent those recommendations differ from the older adult's wishes.

CONSIDER

If (1) the older adult has a power of attorney, (2) the agent under the POA is the perpetrator of abuse, and (3) a successor agent is named in the POA, consider filing a POA proceeding to remove the agent in lieu of guardianship, which would allow the successor agent to act on the older adult's behalf as agent and may prevent the need for guardianship. (Legal Framework, Ch. 5, Section III.A.2.f.)

Legal Framework, Ch. 4, Section II.B.4.

IF THERE IS AN IMMINENT RISK TO THE OLDER ADULT OR THE OLDER ADULT'S PROPERTY, THE COURT MAY APPOINT AN INTERIM GUARDIAN AFTER NOTICE AND HEARING

One of the most important tools available in guardianship to stop the abuse or exploitation of an older adult is interim guardianship. An interim guardian is a temporary guardian appointed by the clerk of superior court prior to an adjudication of incompetence. (G.S. 35A-1101(11).) The purpose of the interim guardianship is to provide temporary protection for a person who requires immediate intervention to address conditions that constitute imminent or foreseeable risk of harm to the person's physical well-being or to the person's estate when there is reasonable cause to believe the person is incompetent. (G.S. 35A-1114(b).) The clerk's order sets forth the interim guardian's powers and duties, which are limited and extend only so far and so long as necessary to meet the conditions necessitating the appointment of an interim guardian. (G.S. 35A-1114(e).)

CONSIDER

If an older adult has a power of attorney and an agent under the POA is the perpetrator of abuse, an interim guardian of the estate or general guardian has the authority to terminate the POA if authorized by the court order appointing the interim guardian. (Legal Framework, Ch. 5, Section III.A.2.f.)

Legal Framework, Ch. 4, Section II.C.3.b.

COURT HOLDS HEARING TO DETERMINE WHETHER THE OLDER ADULT IS INCOMPETENT AND APPOINTS A GUARDIAN

In the incompetency proceeding, the court (or a jury, if a jury trial is requested) determines, based on the evidence presented, whether the older adult is incompetent. (G.S. 35A-1112.) The term "incompetent adult" is defined as an adult or emancipated minor who lacks sufficient capacity to either

- manage his or her own affairs or
- make or communicate important decisions concerning his or her person, family, or property.

The older adult's lack of capacity may be due to a condition such as dementia, mental illness, intellectual disability, autism, inebriety, or another cause or condition. (G.S. 35A-1101(7).) However, evidence of a specific condition or diagnosis is not required for a court to find that an older adult is incompetent, and evidence of a specific condition or diagnosis is not determinative of incompetency. (*Legal Framework,* Ch. 4, Section II.C.)

If the court does not find that an older adult is incompetent, it will dismiss the petition.

If the court finds that an older adult is incompetent, it must appoint a guardian to act on his or her behalf. (G.S. 35A-1120.) The court's role during the guardianship proceeding is to determine the type of guardianship needed by the older adult based on (1) the older adult's capacity, assets, needs, and liabilities and (2) who can most suitably serve as guardian. (G.S. 35A-1212(a).) There are three main types of guardians under North Carolina law: a guardian of the person (GOP), a guardian of the estate (GOE), and a general guardian (GG). (G.S. 35A-1202(10), (9), (7).) In addition, the court has the authority to order a limited guardianship. (G.S. 35A-1212(a).)

After the clerk adjudicates incompetence and appoints a guardian, the guardian appointed under the clerk's order must then qualify with the court to obtain letters. The guardian initiates this process by submitting an application for letters. A critical step in the qualification process involves the posting of a bond. If a GOE or GG is appointed by the clerk, the GOE or GG must post a bond before receiving any property and before the clerk will issue letters of appointment. (G.S. 35A-1230.) A GOP typically does not have to post a bond. After the guardian submits an application for letters and the clerk approves the bond, the guardian takes an oath. If the clerk approves the application, the clerk issues letters. The letters represent and prescribe the guardian's authority to act on behalf of the older adult.

Legal Framework, Ch. 4, Section II.C.

ONCE APPOINTED, THE GUARDIAN HAS A ROLE IN PROTECTING THE ADULT AGAINST ABUSE

Guardianship is a tool that may be used to stop ongoing abuse of an incompetent older adult and to safeguard such adults against future abuse. Once a guardian is appointed, he or she has a duty to take actions, depending on the type of guardianship created, to protect the older adult and the adult's property from abuse.

CONSIDER

If an older adult has a power of attorney and an agent under the POA is the perpetrator of abuse, a guardian of the estate or general guardian has the authority to terminate the POA. (Legal Framework, Ch. 5, Section III.A.2.f.)

Legal Framework, Ch. 4, Section II.D.

COURT OVERSIGHT OF GUARDIANSHIP CAN HELP PROTECT OLDER ADULTS FROM ABUSE BY THE GUARDIAN OR OTHERS

The court retains jurisdiction following the appointment of a guardian and oversees the guardianship as the "ultimate guardian" with the authority to take action to protect the interests of the incompetent older adult. (G.S. 35A-1203; *In re* Matter of Thomas, 290 N.C. 410, 424–25 (1976).) The risk of an adult under guardianship being abused may be mitigated, in part, by effective court oversight of the guardianship. This includes ensuring that the guardian files timely and complete status reports, inventories, and accountings and taking actions to compel reports, when appropriate, which in extreme cases may result in holding the guardian in contempt of court. It also includes holding hearings to address information presented to the court about potential abuse of the older adult, modifying the guardianship when necessary to protect the older adult or better serve the adult's interests, and, in extreme cases, removing the guardian for failing to protect an older adult from abuse or because the guardian is the perpetrator of abuse.

Any interested person (the movant) may file a motion in the cause in the guardianship proceeding before the clerk of superior court to ask the court to modify the guardianship or consider any matter pertaining to the guardianship. (G.S. 35A-1207(a).) The N.C. Administrative Office of the Courts maintains a form "Motion in the Cause to Modify Guardianship" (Form AOC-E-415). If an emergency exists that threatens the physical well-being of an older adult under guardianship or constitutes a risk of substantial injury to an older adult's estate, the movant may request ex parte relief in the motion filed with the clerk. (G.S. 35A-1207(d).) If the clerk finds reasonable cause to believe that an emergency exists, the clerk may enter an ex parte order to address the emergency pending disposition of the matter at a hearing on the motion.

In extreme cases, removal of the guardian and the appointment of a successor guardian by the court may be necessary. There are two types of removal: removal in an emergency, which does not require a hearing, and removal after a hearing. (G.S. 35A-1291; 35A-1290.) The clerk may remove a guardian without a hearing if the clerk finds reasonable cause to believe that an emergency exists that threatens the physical well-being of the older adult or constitutes a risk of substantial injury to the older adult's estate. (G.S. 35A-1291.)

Legal Framework, Ch. 4, Section II.E.

REPORT MADE TO LAW ENFORCEMENT

In almost all situations, a person who suspects that an older adult is being abused, neglected, or exploited is allowed to report those suspicions to law enforcement directly. Some professionals, such as social workers and medical professionals, may be subject to confidentiality laws that limit voluntary reporting. In addition to provisions on voluntary reporting, North Carolina has three mandatory reporting laws that may directly connect to law enforcement.

- Any person who has reason to believe that a disabled adult needs protection from potential abuse, neglect, or exploitation must report these suspicions to DSS, and DSS must share information with the district attorney in certain situations. (G.S. 108A-102.)
- Financial institutions and their officers and employees must make a report to law enforcement if there is reason to suspect that a disabled or older adult (age 65 or over) is the target or the victim of financial exploitation. (G.S. 108A-115.)
- Physicians and hospitals must make a report to law enforcement if they treat wounds, injuries, or illnesses that
  - arise from a gunshot wound, poisoning, knife, or sharp instrument if it appears that a criminal act was involved or
  - cause grave bodily harm or grave illness if it appears that the harm or illness resulted from a criminal act of violence. (G.S. 90-21.20.)

Legal Framework, Ch. 3, Section II.E.1.

LAW ENFORCEMENT INITIATES CRIMINAL INVESTIGATION

A report of suspected elder abuse, neglect, or exploitation may cause a law enforcement agency to initiate a criminal investigation. If, during the investigation, law enforcement has reasonable cause to suspect that a disabled adult was a potential victim of abuse, neglect, or exploitation, it must report it to DSS (unless the original referral or report came from DSS).

CONSIDER

If a report of suspected elder abuse, neglect, or exploitation involves a power of attorney (POA), consider taking a close look at the POA to determine whether a crime may be implicated. Remember that cases involving POAs are not just civil in nature. (Legal Framework, Ch. 5, Sec. III.B.)

Once law enforcement officials have concluded the investigation, they will either close the case or refer it to the district attorney's office for review. The district attorney has the exclusive authority to decide whether to prosecute someone criminally and, if so, with what charges.

Legal Framework, Ch. 3, Section. II.E.

CONSIDER

At this point in the process, think about whether an effort should be made to protect the older adult victim's assets in a financial exploitation case.

Four options to consider:

1. *If a person has been criminally charged with financial exploitation, the prosecutor may ask the court to freeze the defendant's assets. (Legal Framework, Ch. 3, Section III.G.)*
2. *If DSS is conducting an APS evaluation, it can ask the court for an order authorizing the agency to freeze the older adult's assets and inspect financial records. (Ch. 2, Section II.C.3.e.)*
3. *If the older adult victim lacks capacity, DSS may seek guardianship, including interim guardianship. (Ch. 4, Section II.C.3.b.) An interim guardian may, for example, take action to locate and secure assets and obtain financial records to the extent authorized by the court order appointing the interim guardian.*
4. *If the older adult victim has a power of attorney and lacks capacity, DSS may file a POA proceeding to remove the agent under the POA if the agent is the source of the exploitation. (Ch. 5, Section III.A.2.f.)*

FINANCIAL INSTITUTION IDENTIFIES POTENTIAL ELDER ABUSE

A financial institution, such as a credit union or bank, may notice activity involving a customer's account that appears suspicious. Or if the institution has personal contact with the customer, staff may notice behavior or physical signs that suggest potential abuse. If so, the financial institution has three duties to consider: suspicious activity reports, trusted person contacts, and mandatory state reporting.

SUSPICIOUS ACTIVITY REPORT

Financial institutions are required to submit "Suspicious Activity Reports" (SARs) to the Financial Crimes Enforcement Network (FinCEN) within the U.S. Department of the Treasury. With these reports, federal and state law enforcement officials are able to both investigate individual cases and identify trends. A financial institution may be required to file a SAR if it knows, suspects, or has reason to suspect that a transaction conducted or attempted by, at, or through the financial institution

- involves funds derived from illegal activity or attempts to disguise funds derived from illegal activity,
- is designed to evade regulations promulgated under the Bank Secrecy Act (BSA),
- lacks a business or apparent lawful purpose, or
- involves the use of the financial institution to facilitate a criminal activity.

There has been significant growth in the reporting of SARs related to elder financial exploitation since the reporting mandate went into effect in 2013.

Legal Framework, Ch. 7, Section II.E.5.

TRUSTED PERSON CONTACT

Under state law, financial institutions are encouraged to offer disabled adults and older adults an opportunity to submit to the institutions a list of "trusted persons" and to update the lists periodically. (G.S. 108A-114.) If an institution has reasonable cause to believe that an adult is the victim or target of financial exploitation, it must report the suspicion to any "trusted person" identified by the customer, unless the institution "suspects that [the trusted person is] financially exploiting the disabled adult or older adult." (G.S. 108A-115(a)(1).)

Legal Framework, Ch. 7, Section II.F.1.

MANDATORY STATE REPORTING

Financial institutions are subject to several federal and state confidentiality laws that can at times be perceived as barriers to information-sharing. Even with these rigorous laws in place, financial institutions and their officers and employees are clearly allowed to comply with the reporting requirements for adult protective services (APS), law enforcement, "trusted persons," and the federal government (SARs).

- **Duty to report all abuse, neglect, and exploitation to APS.** Financial institutions must comply with the universally mandated APS reporting law, which requires all individuals who have reasonable cause to believe that a disabled adult is in need of services to make a report to DSS. (G.S. 108A-102.)
- **Duty to report financial exploitation to APS.** Financial institutions are also subject to a more-specific (and likely redundant) law that requires them to make a report to APS if they have reasonable cause to believe that a disabled adult is the victim or target of financial exploitation. (G.S. 108A-115(a)(3).)
- **Duty to report financial exploitation to law enforcement.** If a financial institution has reasonable cause to believe that a disabled adult or older adult (age 65 years and older) is the victim or target of financial exploitation, the institution must make a report to local law enforcement. (G.S. 108A-115(a)(2).)

Legal Framework, Ch. 7, Section II.F.